STAYING THE NIGHT

poems by

Ilene H. Rudman

Finishing Line Press
Georgetown, Kentucky

STAYING THE NIGHT

*For my sister A.C. who always
and fervently believed*

*for my friend S.G. for her gifted organizing
skills and artist's eye*

*and my teacher S.B.
who artfully and patiently taught*

Copyright © 2021 by Ilene H. Rudman
ISBN 978-1-64662-666-3   First Edition
All rights reserved under International and Pan-American Copyright Conventions. No part of this book may be reproduced in any manner whatsoever without written permission from the publisher, except in the case of brief quotations embodied in critical articles and reviews.

ACKNOWLEDGMENTS

Grateful acknowledgment is due to the editors of the following publications in which these poems first appeared.

The Comstock Review: "The Darfur Diet," "Listen," "You Say"
Kind of Hurricane Press: "Motor Oil"
Apeiron Review: "Winter Blossoms"
Crab Creek Review: "Relishing"
CALYX: "Sausage"
LEON Literary Review: "Sleep"

Thanks also to: my teacher Suzanne Berger and my fellow poets of a dozen years in her weekly Master Class; to the members of the Black Oak Poet's workshop for their generous feedback; and friend George Whitehead who oh-so-patiently applied his big heart and engineer's brain to the task of being my first reader. Thanks also to: my dear friend and art advisor extraordinaire Sandra Grindlay who helped make a book out of seemingly disparate poems and find the best possible cover; sister Anita Checket who believed in me when I ran out of gas and inspiration; and my cheering longtime friends Linda McGill, Starr Shulman (of blessed memory) and the members of my Women's Group who kept the loving pressure on. This book would also not have been completed without the help of poet/friend Mary Ellen Geer who brought her editor's eye and red pen to this manuscript; or to the generosity of friends Joan Klagsbrun and Julian Miller whose enthusiastic loan of their Berkshire retreat helped make a pile of poems into a manuscript.

Publisher: Leah Huete de Maines
Editor: Christen Kincaid
Cover Art: Michael J. Cassella
Author Photo: © 2020 George A N Whitehead
Cover Design: Sandra Grindlay

Order online: www.finishinglinepress.com
also available on amazon.com

Author inquiries and mail orders:
Finishing Line Press
PO Box 1626
Georgetown, Kentucky 40324
USA

Table of Contents

Waiting for the Light 1
Rebirth 3
Jacob's Ladder 4
Cardiac Blues 5
My Boyfriend Prefers Sleeping with the Dog 6
Sleep 7
Rituals 8
Phantom Rabbit 9
Flying 10
Sausage 11
Small Talk / Maul / Turkeys 12
Two Johns, a Bill and a Bob 13
Motor Oil 15
Urge for Going 16
The Witness at The Hague 17
In the Garden of the Cats 18
February Ice on the Bay of Fundy 19

∽∽

Dreams 21
Mother May I 22
Some Questions One Might Ask the Buddha 24
Easy Love 25
Winter Blossoms 26
Sometimes 27
After 28
My Alpaca 29
The Miller's Daughter 30
The Darfur Diet 31
Brain Matter 32
Relishing 33
Intermission During the Play *We Live in Cairo* 34
On Being a Plus-One 35
You Say 36

Waiting for the Light

Much like the mare
that races in my dreams
white as snow and fast,
my grandmother races
across the paddock
at the edge of my sleep.

It was at my 9th birthday
party that her hair turned
from raven black to snow
white and we knew her time
had speeded up.

My mother thought
there was virtue in hot
water and bleached sheets.
Socks that were snow white
made her weep with gladness.

Oh how I long
in the long hot night of my
mid-life to be a child again
on a snow day when school is called
and the windows are crystalline with
ice, even inside.

For my birthday I visit the florist's
ice-cold room where blooms stay fresh—
drawn inside to the deep red tulips, but choose
instead the calm of the snow white cyclamens
and their tender green leaves.

The eyebrows of Schweitzer and Frost
in their snow white arcs of bristle
across steep foreheads reassure me
that the rhythmic cadence of words
is possible, even now;

even now, when the world turns
gray and cold with fear of the coming
night, even now I dream there are Great
Snowy owls perched on the tops of a
thousand tall pines all across the world
waiting for the light to return.

And so I choose before bed
in evening's last light to read again
the *Snow White Rose Red* story to my
grandmother's unborn great grandchild—
of the bear and his journey and the choices
that are waiting.

Rebirth
> *(for J.R. on father's day)*

after the blue cold
of late March snow
I bought a potted gardenia

cloying, fragrant and creamy with mystery;
and though I remembered the last time
I tried and failed to nurture one

I also remembered
that one week when   oh
its creamy blossoms filled my house
with a leaf green scent of comfort

**

so it was worth it I knew
worth waking before dawn
bone-tired to hold and chant
to my grandson

carrying him tight against my heart
looking together in the mirror
at our morning sharp reflections

***

my wild white hair, haggard eyes
and the large dazzle of his   recognition
oookey fadookey padookey fadookey
I'd greet him each morning

smelling the sweet smell of his
baby skin and the scent of blossoms
about to burst

oookey fadookey
each evening I'd whisper
into his delicate and perfect ears

Jacob's Ladder *
      (for Emily Hillman DeWitt 1946-1996)

Just before death
my sister's arms flew
up   angel wings
in greeting

as if her wish to stay
was stronger than
her body's need
to leave

into the living
room her long-legged
teenaged daughters rolled
her hospital bed so she

whose eyes had mostly
closed could see
the Black Eyed Susans
bow their heavy heads

daughters and daughters'
friends and husband
we all kept watch the rise
and fall   her breath

more gasp than breath 'til
seeming safe to steal a bit
of sleep we went upstairs
in shifts

and somewhere in the darkest
part of night the silence
shifted   and when I came
barefoot down the narrow stairs

I found stillness
and her husband holding
tight   my baby sister's
cooling hand and the cat

who'd woken him just
in time purring on my
sister's still still chest.

Cardiac Blues

Lying still in that blue-cold tunnel, filled
with anti-anxiety drugs, plugged into headphones
with chanting monks and nuns you are told

when to hold your breath, told when to breathe again—
smothered by noise, hammered by fear, determined
to be brave, to do what they say.

*In heart matters there's always a price for
holding your breath, for telling the truth—even when
your father used the belt you held your breath
'till you turned blue and your mother intervened.*

Next they will place an IV
for the Versed to erase your memory
for the anesthesia to hold you under

to be there for potassium to head off complications
too numerous to name; and they will shave your groin
and snake cold catheters into your heart;

*Chances are things could go wrong
in matters of the heart, that he might not be the man
you thought he was, that love was only sex confused
by a bad grasp of history,*

and then snap electrodes onto your back and onto your
front to map the heart's miss-firings, that make you afraid
each time you feel pounding, each time you feel racing—

*when what you really need is to curl
like spoons through the night, your heart entrusted
to a friend who would stay the night if only you were
brave enough to ask.*

My Boyfriend Prefers Sleeping with the Dog

My boyfriend rescued a small white
dog he named Charlie. Charlie has curly
hair and if bigger would look like
a very small lamb.

At my boyfriend's house she starts off the night
in her donut-shaped bed, but somehow finds a way
with her very short legs to wriggle up between
the sheets and his warm body.

I won't, however, let Charlie sleep with us at
my house. I suspect you may think me ungenerous
or even a bit cruel. But I need to tell you
despite Mayo clinic research on the positive

impact of dogs in the bedroom*, that sleeping
with a small white lamb of a dog is impossible.
So, I tell my boyfriend—*you need to choose
sleep with Charlie in my loft on a not-so-*

*comfortable bed or with me on my pillow-
top mattress and leave Charlie downstairs
whimpering.* And though I know your
choosing to spend the night with Charlie

is the wisest choice for all—we know she will
cry and suspect I won't—what neither of us
remember is how much we depend on each
others' warm bodies to rescue us

from the empty beds of childhood.

*"*Out Of The Doghouse and Into The Bed*," New York Times, March 2018.

Sleep

For years I don't try. Round each
day stooped with the lack of it. Pillows

watch me not trying. Attitude matters
little. Prayer is useless. I know there are

decisions to be made. Should the pillows
be recovered? Should the clock's hands be

unwound? Oh, if only I *could*
recover time. Reconfigure its formula.

**

The sleep experts use electrodes to measure. Suggest
ear foam to block sound. Eye shades to block light.

There are tiny pills to break in two.
Things to avoid in the afternoon. Things to do.

Sometimes days pass unnoticed. Sometimes
nights. Time is running on its own

abbreviated schedule. *Hurry* says the clock.
Hurry.

***

But no matter how hard I try
I can't recover what's lost

between dusk and dawn. The figures never
add up. My pillows nod, taking the brunt

tossing and turning as the clock's
cruel hands go round.

Rituals
           (for J.R.)

*Do you remember
the year everyone
seemed to die?*

It was the fall
you turned four
our rituals began—
I would end each day

and conversation with "I love
you."; did it until you said "I
know" and "please stop."

You devised a nighttime ritual—
would ask me how my worrying
was and "is your worry-bar still rusty?"

You pretended to drill
with your still chubby fingers
a hole in the side of my head

and pull out the worry-bar.
"It's rusty again," you always
declared and replaced it
with a stainless steel one
meant to last.

Your drilling went on,
it seemed for years,
till the spring you'd grown
at least 6 inches—

and our rituals stopped.
We had survived it seemed.
Will you remember?

Phantom Rabbit

There is a rabbit who
appears and disappears
each night

with her white-gray tail
she sweeps away sorrows
that keep sleep at bay

I can count on her always

just last night she swept away
your photo tacked to the front
of my fridge with those Renoir magnets

next she swept away
the odd sock you left in the loft
and the argyle pattern I planned to try

then she was ready
to tackle your emails
stacked on my desktop

somehow she's learned to
manage the delete button
with her forepaws

always on her haunches
her pink nose twitches furiously
whenever I think of calling you

if I ignore her insistent
thumping I know she will
scream her terrible rabbit scream.

Flying

It doesn't matter if the large man
in the front seat has pushed himself back
almost into your lap, so close you can see
where his hair follicles begin
and the shiny tight skin beneath.

It doesn't matter if the woman
next to you with the head cold
has commandeered the arm rest
gone through several packs
of Kleenex and insists on sharing
the latest *National Enquirer*.

It's when you're landing the real
trouble begins—when seatbelt signs
come on and trays must be returned
to their full upright position; when there's
one chance left to throw away
what you no longer need—

persistent nightmares about uncertain
love; endless regrets about creative risks
never taken; those worries about your brittle
bones that keep you from hiking the El Camino;

and a phone at home so piercingly silent
even behind shuttered windows
you can hear the mournful honk
of Snow Geese in their vee flying home.

Sausage

I fell in love with Jimmy Dean
pork sausages flying first class
to San Francisco on an airline that
no longer exists. The sausages were
tiny breakfast links with little
bits of string still attached. I was
traveling with my boss to a conference
in Sausalito. We were having a bit
of a flirtation. He was an ex-priest,
married and spoke with a hint of an Irish
brogue. I was 26, Jewish. It all made
some sort of sense. It was, after all,
the 60's. I was still a virgin and had
never had an orgasm nor eaten pork
sausages. And at 26,000 feet I sensed
that if I had to choose, eating sausages
would clearly win.

Small Talk / Maul / Turkeys

Nowhere is rest more needed
than afterwards when talk is.

But talking was what she knew
best, and doing was how he knew.

How she could be somebody;
how he could be and be with.

Maul

What if what we own can't be
passed down, though we try?

But trying isn't the same as
chopping enough stove wood.

The cord of wood she needed
split. Axe against wedge.

Wedge against maul. Window
cracked to let night air.

Turkeys

Every year the girl and her father
sold turkeys at the turkey

farm. She butchered the Toms
her father hosed down the cement.

Don't know if he really was her father
or if ever the girl married.

What if we got it all wrong?

Two Johns, a Bill and a Bob

That's what Match.com is serving up
grown men who live in rented rooms
who have beer bellies
wear muscle shirts and gold chains
around turkey necks and who "promise"
they are trying to stop smoking.

Men who say they're 5'9 (and never are)
who say they exercise 5 times a week and never do
who claim a degree in linguistics but can't spell
and want a lady who's as "comfortable in jeans
as in a little (always little) black dress."

Men who look "at least ten years"
younger than their age
who like to hold hands
walk beaches at sunset
know how to treat a woman "right"
and want that woman to be at least
ten years their junior.

Men who have heavy tuition bills
for children still in college
or great relationships with their adult children
who invariably live thousands of miles away.

**

Whom should I pick?

Perhaps the aging never-married
Charleston poet or the venture capitalist
addicted to Nicorette?

Would I be better off with
the political conservative who
claims to have marched in Selma
the soybean farmer from Missouri
whose wife died just a month before
or the Civil War historian (so Google
reports) charged by the FBI for stealing
rare books from the Library of Congress?

So many wounded hearts
coming at me through the ether
I am left breathless at my choices.

***

What if I described myself like my 1994 Lexus
a bit outdated but classy with elegant leather seats
beginning to wear   that's sturdy on the road
but some major repair work is needed?

Who would I attract?

Perhaps a Chevy Nova needing a paint job
with an air freshener that smells like Lysol
and a pair of fuzzy dice hanging from the rear-
view mirror—lady luck seen coming and going.

Motor Oil

you require high test
says the kid at Jiffy Lube
eyeing my '94 Lexus
its matted carpet
and cracked leather seats

but I simply drive to work
to shop and back   and then
I get it—it's not the miles I drive
but the years I've traveled
the scant mileage that remains

Monday, Lou my lover
from a time of lower mileage
emailed from Santa Fe an
image of our sky-blue Corolla
turning 300,000 miles

there's much to learn
from a man who knows
how to keep a car running
even in desert conditions

Urge for Going*
    after Mark Strand

Why did you travel?
    Because I had no choice.
Why did you travel?
    Because the walls were too close and I needed to breathe.
What did you wear?
    My best coat and a false smile.
What did you wear?
    The first thing I found in the closet that wasn't stained
    with tears and the memory of tears.
Who did you sleep with?
    Anyone with a packed suitcase and a sense of humor.
Anyone?
    If you must know, I only remember the ones who made
    me laugh and lasted more than a night.
Why did you lie to me?
    Because I had no choice and the truth might kill what time hasn't.
Why are you going?
    Because time's become the enemy and the horizon's much too close.
How long should I wait for you?
    I don't know— I won't know until I know.
How long should I wait?
    Until your longing outstrips your impatience.

**Poem title after a song by Joni Mitchell*

The Witness at The Hague

I tried. I did. Failed. Tried
again. About the leather
boots and broken sticks

and rifle butts you need
the truth. There was no hoax.
But civil war and bodies. Rapes.

No hoax. Not mannequins.
Many bodies. Women's bodies.
Fleeing children I led across.
To safe arms, I hoped. I had to

help. And caught yes. And
herded into camp. Yes.
With local women. Captured.
Broken. Our hands, our feet.

Stomped on again again again.
But only my body. They raped.
My body only. Not my will.
Not my spirit. Can you

understand? Will you judge?
Will you jury? I the only one
with words and means.
I had to tell. I had no choice.

You need to know. A starless night.
I had no choice. Found fence and sky.
Escaped, I did. The only one
who could and did. I left behind

the others. Women. Women without.
Words. Means. I had to leave.
I had to come. I had no choice.
I had the means. The words.
The truth.

In the Garden of the Cats

Listen, do not imagine I don't know
    what you are imagining—
        that it's your own shadow

straying outside the gates of the crematorium
    seeking the garden of the cats—
        smell of urine drawing you

towards the mounds
    where you buried
        the strays you shot.

You never strayed far
    (though I wish you had)
        from our home—

the home across the street
    from the garden with its
        bone-made crosses

guarding each mound. Your ghost
    each evening mounting and descending,
        descending and mounting our stairs.

Is the sound I listen for you or your footsteps
    stalking the cats or me stalking
        the garden of your memory?

February Ice on the Bay of Fundy

I believe trees
understand more than priests
and a ring around the moon
doesn't always mean
the sun's going to shine.

I believe that telling
a lover the truth
about all your old lovers
or even momentary indiscretions
won't always be well-received
and that some truths are
best left unsaid.

I believe that silk sheets
and flannel gowns make
for a good night's sleep
but that sometimes in deep winter
even sleep isn't enough.

I believe that some words
like *ichor* or *agape* or even *segue*
are best left for Scrabble
and that you have suffered
enough for at least two lifetimes.

I believe there's a level of pain
that can't be touched in each of us
and the way you watch over me
when you think I'm sleeping
can melt even February ice
on the Bay of Fundy.

〜〜 〜〜
〜〜 〜〜

Dreams

like potatoes. Their peels saved for soup.
Peels saved for compost. Some of them
pockmarked. Others blighted. All have eyes.

They see you through winter.
Blue endless winter. Stored in
your cellar. Clogged and

untethered. You want to forget
them. Need to forget them.
Always you are hungry for

Yukon golds or Red garnets—
doesn't much matter. Boil them till they
soften. Bake them till they soften.

Their eyes will still be watching.

  **

You dream of lost closets.
Found where you left them.

Unhinged and unlocked.
Abandoned prom dresses,

shoes without tongues and
coats without arms.

Arms you've been missing. Forgot
you'd been missing. Wrapped so

tightly. Round your waist. Round your
chest. So much you've wasted.

Your clothes and your secrets.
Moth-eaten hours and motherless dreams.

Mother May I

go to where I can
touch lick brush up against
anything or anyone
that just might

might I buy enough
paper towels and toilet
paper, basmati brown
rice and sweet potatoes
without worrying if

if without a mask
something Bad might
happen   should I
walk next to   too
close to someone
any one who might
spit or sneeze or cough
or unknowingly harbor
what

what will happen mother
if I open door latches or
turn handles that have
not been rubbed or sprayed
scrubbed or bleached

or hoard masks meant
for people who for a
living work to keep
my neighbors from dying?

***

Mother might things improve if
I stopped listening to false news or
true news that morphs faster than
any virus   if I stop

stop gorging on news and sent instead
cards I bought for missed birthdays   if

I tackle my piles of paper and throw

throw away food six months
beyond expiration   if I arrange
books by author and size and make
piles of clothes for Goodwill

if for good measure I return to
my loom and weave yesterday's
yarn into fabric that holds
might

might we mother oh mother
find our way   back   home again?

Some Questions One Might Ask the Buddha

If wild turkeys with their prehistoric
heads hunting for grubs be the dreams
of my neighbor, should I send
for help?

If I'm looking for a roadmap
on how to return home again
after so many years away
will an app on my phone
be the best option?

If the kisses my ex-husband's wife
give me after Thanksgiving turkey
be signs of dementia, would returning
her kisses be a curse or a kindness?

If my questions are only energy
looking for direction
will putting them on the page
let me live more fully
between the commas
and the periods?

If words are only life forms
looking for a home
can I, with this poem,
give them sanctuary?

Easy Love

I shall never grow old
with a man who knew my body
young and eager, never have a lover
who remembers getting tangled in the covers
and my legs, caught between satin and passion.

I will never grow old with
a man who knew my nipples
rosy and erect or my hair
waist-length as it came
undone in love.

And now when I'm more
gray than not with a body
no longer pliant I wonder
will he see only what is
and not what was and on those
mornings after yet another
fight of tangled words
I worry will the present
be enough.

How far back must memory
travel to ground the present
make safe the future; how much
history of easy love do we need
to help us bear the fading?

Winter Blossoms
      (for C.O. 1941-2015)

I wouldn't blame you
for walking away—you said
it's the wise thing to do

and I picture you in your
White Mountain cabin
surrounded by oil paints, easel

and the gamey sweet smell
of an apple wood fire
and I think about whether

I should or could—veering
between wanting to try
for what we started

and wanting as you advised
to run—*run away from*
falling in love with a man

whose cells are running amok
tomorrow I will send you
an overlarge box of Belgian truffles

and a dozen Narcissus
the kind guaranteed to grow
fastest from bulb to bloom.

Sometimes
    (for G.W.)

happiness arrives disguised as
the lovely bones of a small and tender
field mouse in the talons of a Great Horned owl

sometimes it catches you by surprise
like the time you both repeated by heart
lines from "The Walrus and the Carpenter"

once it arrived on a July-
hot morning when he brought
you a cup of Sumatra in one

of his grandmother's cracked porcelain
cups and some wild Maine blueberries in bed
his broad hands still wet

from the rinsing—but when he
made for you and your poems
a perfectly quiet room small

desk and much light there was so
much happiness it was almost
more than you could bear.

After
          (for G.A.G. 1946-2006)

buzz or hiss
uncertain which
flames or toast
sunday crackle
a lamp or faucet
perhaps rain drumming

folding chairs refolded
candles lit relit
no tears left
the mourners gone
their warm bodies
gone all gone

in symbols or syllables
the dead speak
sometimes they tap
sometimes they whisper
cups move and saucers
there is only silence

not even your whisper

I listen I listen

My Alpaca

Your Modigliani neck, baby face
button black eyes and cream white coat

that clucking—clicking suction sound you make—
it's all I can do not to jump your fence.

Though I call you mine, you and your dusty-gray
brothers belong to the strange man with the small

house and big tractor along the stony path
to the Wildlife Sanctuary. He says he bought

you for your wool—that he's learning to shear it
and card it and sell it. He has seen us talking

as I pass you on my hikes. Once
he invited me inside to view your

wool strewn across fleece skirting tables
and lodged in fine-toothed combs awaiting spinning.

I do not trust this man. He moved large boulders
with his pickup truck to block cars from the Sanctuary.
(I think I saw some rifles inside.)

He claims Park Rangers made him do it. They say
they did not. I do not trust his intent for you or your family.

I read in last week's paper *"*Alpaca, it's what's for dinner:
restaurants serve up alternatives to the usual beef and chicken.*"

The poster chef for unusual meats, Dave Larksworthy, says
his favorite is Alpaca. Your owner insists he's breeding
you only for your wool—perhaps I should be afraid.

*Atlanta Magazine (October 28, 2014)

The Miller's Daughter

I didn't know what my father did not tell me
about gold and straw.

I didn't know the spin he put to the king
on what I could do with a spinning wheel.

So, you'll understand, I hope, when the manikin offered help,
I overlooked his size, his stilts, the strange gleam in his small eyes.

He knew what to do with a wheel,
so I gave him my jewels and took what he offered.

I had no choice.

All night the wheel whirred
and reels of straw were full of gold when dawn broke.

Three nights I watched
as he saved my life from the greedy king.

Of course I promised my first born to this small man.
You would do the same, if fate had placed you in that room.

No matter we hadn't exchanged names;
his rumpled shirt, the stilts he used to reach my door,
the feel of hot straw against my skin were what I knew.

Months passed.

I wed my captor, bore his child and rarely thought of the tiny man
who saved my life and promises made during frantic nights.

But nights when sleep won't come, I remember how time passed
in that locked room, sparks from the wheel, the heady smell of straw;

the soft corner where I lay half sleeping,
the feel of gnarled fingers lifting my skirt
and the pushing and kneading of his small hands.

The Darfur Diet*

First they set before us
their largest trays with chipped
and missing plates and cups; then

we were told to drink
the empty glasses of orange
juice and Abre they offered
to wash down the chunks of lamb
and chicken already gnawed
to the bone by war-
smart rats.

Next they said
we should feast on what remained
of what was no longer fit
for the women or the women's

children; said the women must
fight for the bones left by the afore-mentioned
rats, women who, if truth be told, (and let us
pray some day it will) have been known
to kill for these bones whose
marrow might still be

full of life
to be sucked by their
babies who have already forgotten
their sucking reflex, yes

*in times of plenty the just shall
go hungry; in times of hunger the just
shall eat headlines.*

*The ritual of hospitality is as important in the Sudan as in other Arab and African countries, from the African Studies Center, University of Pennsylvania

Brain Matter

Some people eat brains. Your mother
did. Your boyfriend does. Pigs, squirrels

horses, cattle, monkeys, chickens,
fish, lamb and goats' brains.

They claim they're a delicacy.
French restaurants serve them with garlic

and lots of butter. They're expensive
and ugly and cousins to calves'

tongue and Kishke—blood sausage stuffed
with things you don't wish to know about.

In a funereal ritual of the Fore people
of New Guinea, those close to the deceased

eat their brains to create a sense of immortality.
Perhaps you should try some.

Relishing

Last night my ex-husband's wife kissed me.
        It was on the sofa in the playroom shortly after
                she tasted my raw cranberry orange relish

at my son and daughter-in-law's Thanksgiving.
        Perhaps it was the orange zest I'd added.
                A chaste kiss. Innocent but still

full-hearted. It may have been that after
        thirty years of flint gray silence she'd decided
                we were some sort of sisters—

married to a man whose heart had started
        to fail. I didn't ask. I didn't need to know.
                Fifteen years my junior, she was already

starting to fade. Perhaps, I thought, I could learn
        to love this woman who stole my husband,
                wandering the night in her long winter coat.

Intermission during the Play *We Live in Cairo*

You take your stretch between
acts, a well-educated Cambridge
woman seeking white wine and mints

standing in line checking for familiar
faces, engaged in the play of a revolution
long in coming. Lights already

blinking, you follow the arrows
to *Restrooms*—and find a line
of doors with small signs

saying *gender neutral*; and although
you'll admit to a moment's hesitation
you think "okay, I'm okay with this

no longer radical concept." And enter
a white room with 5 closed stalls and
5 open urinals and wonder if

you've made some major faux pas—
what if it's only meant for LGBTQ
folks and not a 70-year-old heterosexual

woman and ask the other occupant if
you've made a mistake—they smile
and shake their head "no" and you realize

you're not as hip as you think—and how it
must have felt for so many over so many
years to never know if they belonged;

and how the fight for gender neutral
bathrooms and the Cairo uprising might
have more in common than you ever imagined

On Being a Plus-One

I need to tell you that being
a plus-one at the wake of your
boyfriend's dead wife's ex-husband

was complicated—there were no
helpful hints in etiquette books on
whether or not to introduce yourself

to the grieving husband. It was like
being Nancy Drew investigating family
secrets—rough cut and disparate puzzle

pieces falling into place
amidst sepia photos and tiny
watercress and radish sandwiches.

And though I managed to escape
awkward eye contact through several
unnecessary bathroom trips—

still I was just a plus-one imagining
myself a minus-one at my own wake
wondering if any of my old

boyfriends with their own plus-ones
would attend and what they would say—
and how in the meantime I might

master the art of being awake.

You Say
after a line from Tomas Tranströmer

the lake is a window into the earth and what
emerges from the lake is shadow and fish.
There are depths the lake has yet to disclose
and what we think of as carp and sole are really

fragments of sailors lost in the storms and
what appears only as shadows can choose
in a moment to take form and

I say the sky is a cover for the day. Today's
messages were brought by carrier pigeons. In
the cloudless sky they form rings of gray-white
feathers. Halos looking for heads. Whatever lies

ahead is foretold in scraps of damp paper clutched
in their claws. Compass. Lamplight. Maps.
Enough for me to go by.

www.ingramcontent.com/pod-product-compliance
Lightning Source LLC
LaVergne TN
LVHW041557070426
835507LV00011B/1146